Speech Help for Toddlers

I0163128

By Camila Philbin

*Please keep in mind that articulation errors can be a normal part of development for toddlers, but some children might need additional help. Practice and repetition are both extremely important for children who have a speech delay.

ISBN: 978-1-257-13241-6

Basic Word Book

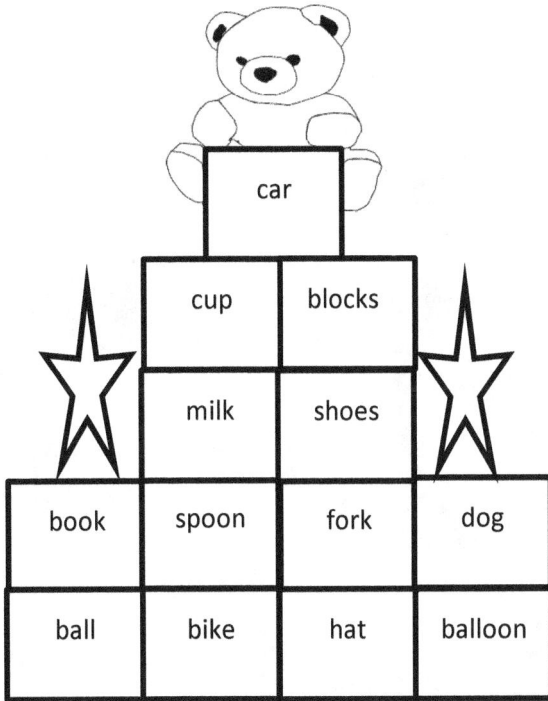

	car	
cup	blocks
milk	shoes
book	spoon	fork	dog
ball	bike	hat	balloon

Read this *Basic Word Book* to your toddler (at least once a day). Once your toddler is familiar with these words, encourage your toddler to read this book to you. Write your toddler's name on the blank lines provided. Help your child to say, recognize, and eventually spell his or her name. Pause when you get to the bold word on each page, and encourage your toddler to say the word. Asking questions after each page will also help improve vocabulary.

Would _____
like to ride in
this **car**?

What is in the **cup**?

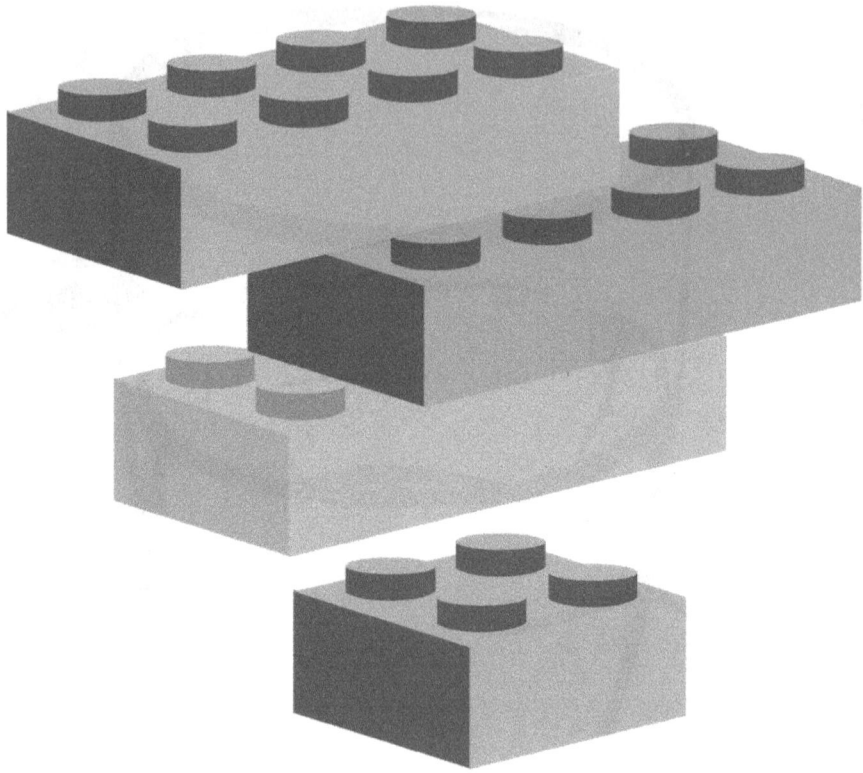

What can
_____ build
with these
blocks?

Do you like to drink **milk** with your cookies?

Can _____
run fast in
these **shoes**?

I like to read **books**. What books do you like to read?

What would _____ eat with this **fork** and **spoon**?

Would _____ like to play with this **dog?**

Can _____
kick this **ball**
far?

Would _____
like to ride
this **bike**?
Where would
you go?

Is that a funny **hat** on the dog's head?

Do you
want to
play with one
of his
balloons?

My P, B, N, H, and W Beginning and Ending Sounds

This book focuses on beginning and ending sounds that children should be able to vocalize approximately by the age of three. Not all children develop the same, and your toddler may not master these sounds in this order: /p/, /b/, /n/, /h/, and /w/.

Parent Help: This is a description of how these consonant sounds are produced.

/p/   Put your lips together tightly and let the air build up in your mouth. Let a quick burst of air pop out from your lips.

/b/   Put your lips together tightly, and let the air build up in your mouth. Let your voice bellow out from behind your lips.

/n/   Put your tongue behind your front teeth. Let your voice come out through your nose.

/h/   Open your mouth slightly. Push out a quick breath through your throat.

/w/   Pucker your lips, but do not close them all the way. Let your voice come out of your lips as you open them a little more.

P

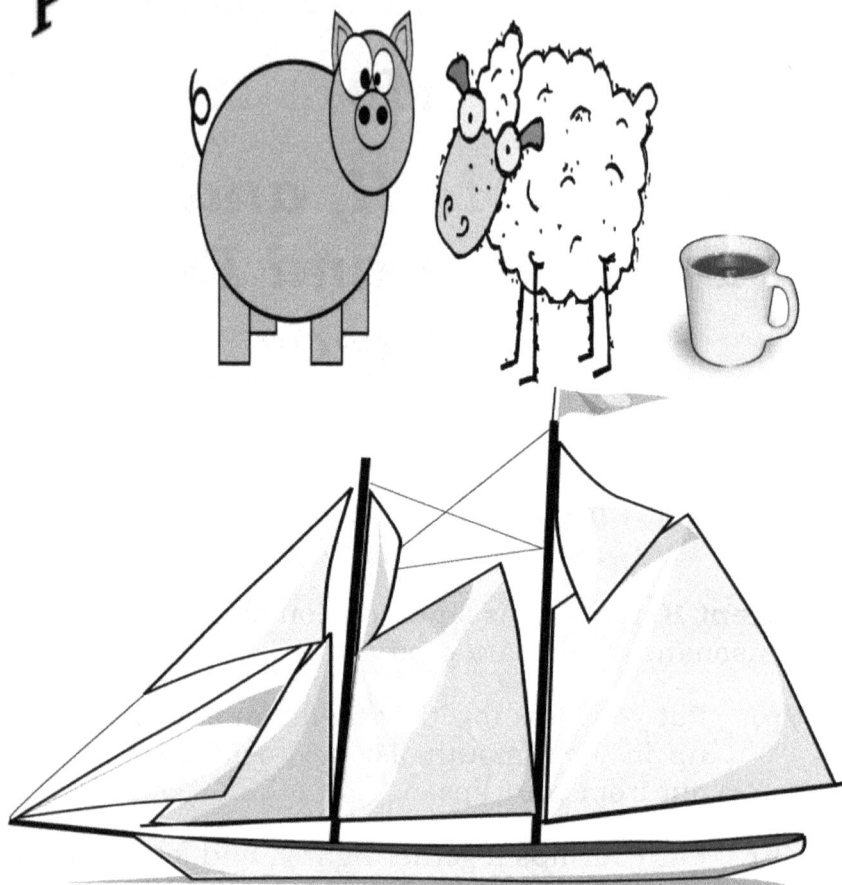

Do you think the **pig,
sheep,** and **cup** will fit
in the **ship**? I hope it
doesn't **tip** over!

H

I **hope** the **heart** covers up the **hole** on the snowman's **hat**.

B

Should we put the **bird**,
bug, and **bag** in the **tub**
together?

Why did the baby **whine**? He **wanted** his bottle of **water** and did not feel **well**.

N

The **train** picked up the
nice man and took him
to **town**. The **sun** was
bright, so the **man** wore
sunglasses.

☆Additional Activities

Cut out the flashcards in the back of this book, and have your child match them to the correct picture on each page.

Play hide-n-seek with the flashcards. Have your child name the cards when they are found.

Tape each flashcard to the wall. Have your child throw a ball at each word and say the word.

Have your child place each flashcard on a spoon. Your child can say the word and then feed it to a doll or stuffed animal.

Tape each word to the ground and have your child roll a toy car over each word. Have your child name the cards that he/she rolls over.

Tape the pictures on the wall and have your child shine a flashlight on each word and say it.

Lay the flashcards on the ground and have your child blow bubbles at each picture. Your child has to say the word each time the bubble pops on the word.

Make a mailbox. Have your child play mailperson and say each word as he/she delivers it to you.

★Additional Websites and Books

The following are websites and books that I have found helpful:

www.starfall.com
This is an interactive website that is great for letters, sounds, and reading.

www.speech-language-therapy.com
This is a website that has free printable pictures for different target sounds.

www.mommyspeechtherapy.com
This website provides free printable pictures and techniques for improving speech.

Brown Bear, Brown Bear, What Do You See? by Bill Martin Jr./Eric Carle
This book encourages talking and child participation.

Ten Apples Up on Top by Dr. Seuss
This book provides lots of repetition and is good practice of the /p/ sound.

The Foot Book by Dr. Seuss
This book provides lots of repetition and is good practice of the /t/ sound.

The Gingerbread Man by Jim Aylesworth
This book provides lots of repetition and is good practice of the /n/ sound.

Flashcards

car

blocks

milk

shoes

books

cup

fork and spoon

dog

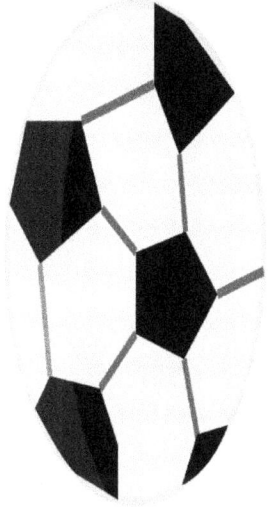

ball

bike

hat

balloons

pig

sheep

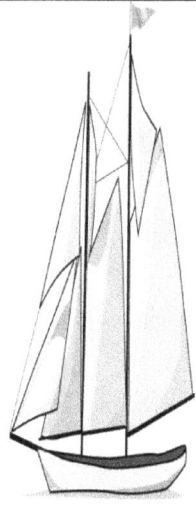

ship

sun

heart

bird

		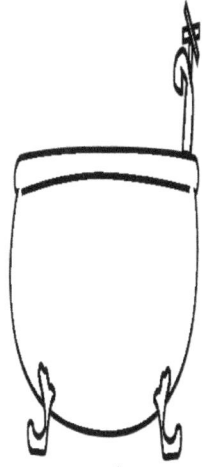
bag	**bug**	**tub**
	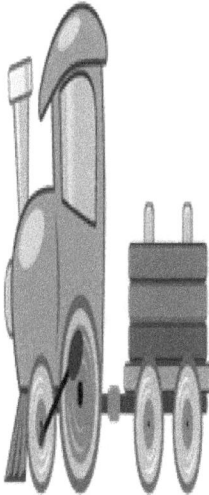	
man	**train**	**bottle of water**

www.ingramcontent.com/pod-product-compliance
Lightning Source LLC
Chambersburg PA
CBHW060106050426
42448CB00011B/2637